W9-APN-639

OUR WILDLIFE WORLD

KANGAROOS

Bill Ivy

Grolier

FACTS IN BRIEF

Classification of kangaroos

Class:	*Mammalia* (mammals)
Order:	*Marsupialia* (pouch-bearing animals)
Family:	*Macropodidae* (kangaroo family)
Subfamilies:	*Macropodinae* (kangaroos)
	Potorinae (rat kangaroos)
Genus:	There are 17 genera of kangaroos.
Species:	There are over 50 species of kangaroos.

World distribution.   Kangaroos are found in Australia, New Guinea and on nearby islands.

Habitat.   Varies with species.

Distinctive physical characteristics.   Most kangaroos have large back paws, small front paws and a large tail. The females have a pouch in which they carry their young.

Habits.   Most live in groups, moving about by hopping on their large back paws and feeding from dusk to dawn.

Diet.   Most eat mainly grass.

Published originally as
"Getting to Know . . . Nature's Children."

This series is approved and recommended by the Federation of Ontario Naturalists.

Canadian Cataloguing in Publication Data

Ivy, Bill, 1953-
  Kangaroos

(Our wildlife world)
Includes index.
ISBN 0-7172-2639-5

1. Kangaroos—Juvenile literature.
I. Title.   II. Series.

QL737.M35I88 1989   j599.2   C89-094706-6

Contents

When the English explorer Captain James Cook was in Australia in 1770, he saw a strange animal unlike anything he had ever seen before. It was almost as tall as he was and had a deer-like head with long ears. The animal had short forearms and a very long tail and it carried its young in a pouch on its stomach. Not only that, it stood upright and hopped around on its two strong hind legs! Can you guess what Captain Cook saw? Right—it was a kangaroo!

Today almost everyone is familiar with this unusual animal. However, there are a lot of interesting kangaroo facts you might not know. For example, did you know that some kangaroos are no larger than a rabbit and that others live in trees? To learn more about these fascinating animals, read on. Kangaroos are full of surprises.

Meet the amazing kangaroo—
Australia's national animal.

Marsupials

Animals whose young are fed and cared for in their mother's pouch are called *marsupials*. Kangaroos are the largest of these pouched animals, but they're not the only ones. Other marsupials include wombats, numbats, bandicoots, koalas, Tasmanian devils and opossums. Except for opossums, which are found in the Americas, all marsupials live in Australia, New Guinea and islands in that area.

These animals have pouches because their young are born premature: their eyes, back legs and tail are not developed yet, and each one is only about the size of a jellybean! Since the baby marsupial is not ready to meet the world, it needs time to feed and grow in a warm, safe environment. Its mother's pouch is the perfect place.

Although rock wallabies usually spend the day in caves, this mother and joey are out basking in the sun.

Living Down Under

Kangaroos live in the wild in Australia, New Guinea and on nearby islands. A few species have been introduced to New Zealand and the red-necked wallaby has been introduced to the United Kingdom. Depending on the type, a kangaroo may live in desert, swamp or forest areas, among rocks or cliffs or high up in trees.

Describing a typical kangaroo is not easy since they come in a variety of sizes, shapes and colors. Let's look at a few of the different types of kangaroo.

Opposite page:
Rock wallabies are much smaller than gray and red kangaroos.

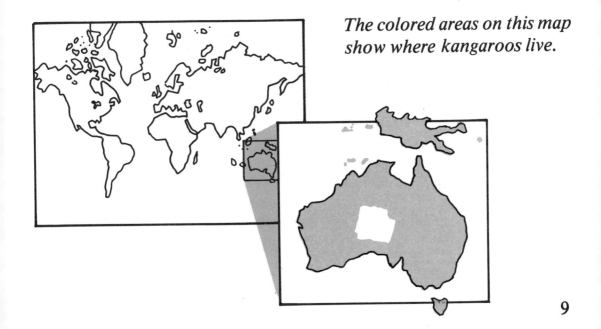

The colored areas on this map show where kangaroos live.

Big Red

Meet "big red," the tallest of the kangaroos. Often standing almost 2 metres (7 feet) tall, red kangaroos can easily look over an average person's head. They weigh up to 90 kilograms (198 pounds). Most male reds have reddish fur similar in color to that of a deer, but the females are usually a blue-gray color. They weigh less than the males and can travel faster. This has earned them the nickname "blue fliers." In some areas, however, the females are red and the males are bluish-gray.

The red kangaroo lives on grasslands and inland plains. During the mating season the male secretes a red substance on his throat and chest. He then rubs this on his back with his forepaws, dyeing the fur an even brighter red. Supposedly this added color impresses the females.

This red kangaroo looks very relaxed, but let there be the least hint of danger and it will be off like a shot.

The Great One

The great gray kangaroo is the heavyweight of its family and the largest of all marsupials. This is the kangaroo you are most likely to see at the zoo. Although it is not always as tall as the red kangaroo, it is usually stronger and heavier.

The Eastern gray kangaroo lives in open forests on the east coast of Australia. Its soft fur ranges in color from mainly gray to brown and its tail has a black tip. The Western gray kangaroo, which is a dark, muddy gray, is found on the west coast. These large kangaroos communicate with a number of sounds including clucks, coughs and loud growls.

Like most of their relatives, gray kangaroos feed mainly on grass.

Middleweights

Most small- to medium-sized members of the kangaroo family are known as wallabies. They have larger feet (in relation to their size), a more hairy tail and smaller front teeth than other kangaroos. They weigh anywhere from 1.8 to 22 kilograms (4 to 50 pounds).

Some wallabies are named for their habitats. Rock wallabies live in caves. Brush wallabies live in areas covered in small trees and shrubs.

Other species are named for one of their physical traits or habits. Hare wallabies are about the same size as hares, behave like them in some ways and can bound with incredible speed. The nail-tailed wallaby has a scale like a small fingernail at the tip of its tail, and the pretty face wallaby . . . well, you get the idea.

This wallaby almost seems to be posing for the photographer.

Walla-Who?

If you take the word wallaby and mix it with the word kangaroo you get "wallaroo." This is the name for a kind of kangaroo that is smaller than the great grays and reds but larger than the wallabies. Wallaroos are often mistaken for their larger relatives, but there are visible differences. Wallaroos are sturdier and have shorter legs. Also called euros or hill kangaroos, they make their home among rocky outcrops and gullies. Their fur is long and coarse and ranges in color from reddish brown to dark blue gray.

Wallaroos can survive on land with little vegetation and very little water as long as there are places such as caves where they can hide from the heat. If they get thirsty they dig in the ground for water with their forepaws. They can dig as deep as one metre (3 feet)!

Some wallaroos have been known to go without water for more than a month.

Above the Rest

You wouldn't think to look for a kangaroo in a tree but that's exactly where tree kangaroos make their home. These kangaroos are built differently than their ground-dwelling cousins. Their front and hind limbs are about the same length and the nails on their front feet are long and curved—ideal for climbing. The soles of their wide, short feet are covered with rough cushion-like pads that prevent them from slipping. Their long tail provides balance for climbing and jumping.

The tree kangaroo is an excellent climber and quite an acrobat. It jumps nimbly from branch to branch and can leap 18 metres (50 feet) to the ground. Once on land it moves along by hopping quickly.

Tree kangaroos live mainly in rain forests. They tend to spend the day in the trees eating leaves and fruit, coming down at night to feed on the herbs that are only available on the ground. But should an enemy appear, they quickly head back to the safety of the tree.

Opposite page:
To reach the ground, tree kangaroos will jump or climb down tail first.

Rat Packs

At first glance it is hard to believe that rat kangaroos are kangaroos at all. In fact, they are so different from the others that they have their own branch on the kangaroo family tree.

There are ten kinds of rat kangaroos and the largest is about the size of a rabbit. They generally live alone in a variety of habitats and feed on roots, insects, fungi and worms. During the day some types sleep in nests of grass which they gather with their tail. One species, the boodie, even sleeps in an underground burrow. The musky rat kangaroo, the smallest of all the kangaroos, has a hairless, scaly tail, five toes on each foot and often walks on all fours.

As its name indicates, the musky rat kangaroo has a strong musky smell.

By Leaps and Bounds

You will never see a kangaroo run. Instead it bounces along on its powerful back legs, using its long tail for balance. While the bigger kangaroos usually travel at about 20 kilometres (12 miles) an hour, they can go well over twice that fast for short distances. When moving at top speed, a red or a great gray can easily leap 8 metres (25 feet) with each hop, as if it had springs in its feet. And one jump can take it as high as a basketball hoop, although most of the time they only jump about half that high.

How does the kangaroo do it? Inside each leg is a tendon, like a large elastic band, which attaches the powerful leg muscle to the bone. When the kangaroo lands its legs bend, stretching this tendon tight and causing the muscle to contract. On its next jump the leg muscle stretches and the tendon snaps back to its original size. This propels the kangaroo forward.

Although kangaroos do a lot of hopping, that's not the only way they get from place to place. Sometimes, including when they graze, they move around slowly on all fours.

Big Foot

Members of the main kangaroo family are known as *macropods*, a word that means big feet. The kangaroo certainly deserves its name. Depending on the species, its feet can be up to 45 centimetres (18 inches) long.

Most kangaroos have only four toes, the big toe having disappeared in all but the musky rat kangaroo. As well, the second and third toes are joined together, forming a "twin toe" that the kangaroo uses to comb its fur. The fourth toe is the largest and provides the most support for the body. It has two nails close together that serve as tweezers for removing pesky ticks.

Compared to its back paws, the kangaroo's front paws are very small and have five fingers. Unlike you, the kangaroo can't bring its thumb around to meet its fingers, so it can't grasp things easily.

Can you guess what kind of wallaby this is? It's a pretty face wallaby.

Life with the Mob

A herd of kangaroos is called a mob. The average mob contains 10 to 20 members. It is usually made up of males, or boomers, females, or does, and young of all ages. Each mob is led by an "old man," the strongest and usually the largest boomer.

A kangaroo mob is a rather loose-knit group. Some members may join the gang for only a few days while others may stay for years. The only real bonds that exist are between a mother and her young.

Mobs are usually on the move searching for food and water. In general, kangaroos prefer to feed from dusk to dawn, but in the cooler winter months they may also feed during the day. Kangaroos are fairly sociable and it is not unusual to see many mobs sharing the same turf.

A mob of gray kangaroos on the alert.

Food Processor

Most kangaroos eat mainly grass, although they will gladly add any other green plant they come across to their menu. Often the grass they eat is not the nice soft type you find on your lawn. Some of it is quite coarse, but this is not a problem for the kangaroo. Its two lower front teeth jut forward like scissor blades for snipping off grass and small twigs.

Like cows, sheep and goats, kangaroos do not digest their food all at once. They swallow it, then later bring it back into their mouth as cud for more chewing. The food is finally digested when the kangaroo is resting. Only the musky rat kangaroo, which eats mainly insects and worms, does not need to break its food down this way.

Most kangaroos must drink water regularly and therefore like to feed near streams or waterholes.

There's nothing like a cool refreshing drink on a hot day!

Stop, Look and Listen

If you tried to sneak up on a kangaroo, you would probably be wasting your time. Kangaroos are very shy and so they are always on the alert. In fact, they never seem to relax completely, not even when they're sleeping. Mostly, they take short naps, getting up often to look, listen and sniff for danger.

Should there be anything at all threatening around, the kangaroo will likely detect it since it has very keen senses. Those big dark brown eyes can see far into the distance, and the large rounded ears can be turned in any direction to pick up even the faintest sounds, wherever they are coming from. Kangaroos also seem to have an excellent sense of smell.

"Follow me!"

Clean Living

Keeping clean is important to a kangaroo. It removes ticks and fleas with its forepaws or with the claws on its second and third toes. You may be surprised to learn that a kangaroo cleans its coat just like your pet cat does. It licks its front paws and runs them over its fur to remove dirt and smooth down the hairs. Joeys get help with their grooming from their mother. A daily bath with mom's tongue keeps them clean.

Some types of kangaroos may even take a bath in a river or lake to wash themselves. The smaller varieties are often quite good swimmers while the larger ones are more awkward in the water.

Kick Boxing

Kangaroos are usually gentle animals—until two males are interested in the same female or an "old man's" authority is challenged by another male. Then there is only one way to settle the disagreement—a boxing match!

Round one begins with a loud cough. Next the two combatants strut stiffly, sizing each other up and waiting for an opening. Standing on their hind legs, they begin to throw punches. As the battle heats up they may lean on their tails and kick with one or both feet. Each boxer must be careful to avoid its opponent's sharp claws. Sometimes one kangaroo may pick up the other and toss him through the air!

While most fighting ends without either animal coming to any harm, injuries do sometimes occur.

Overleaf:
Getting ready to throw the first punch.

Dingo Danger

Life can be dangerous for the kangaroo. The young are the most vulnerable and must always be on the lookout for pythons, large lizards and birds of prey. But the greatest danger of all to young and old alike is the dingo, Australia's wild dog.

At the first sign of danger a kangaroo may stamp its feet or give a loud warning call. Immediately other nearby kangaroos scatter in all directions. Although kangaroos would rather run away than fight, they will defend themselves if cornered, striking out with their big strong feet and sharp toenails. A kangaroo's kick can kill a dingo instantly.

If there is any hint of danger, the joey stays very close to its mother.

G'day, Mate!

Different species of kangaroos mate at different times of the year. In the case of some wallabies, for instance, the mating season is very short and most of the babies are born in late January. Gray kangaroos, on the other hand, are capable of mating anytime during the year. However, they tend to time things so that the young are born in summer and leave the pouch the following spring.

When a female kangaroo is ready to mate, a male will follow her, pawing at her tail. Males compete for the females—often the largest and strongest male will mate with the doe. In fact, in a mob, one male—often the "old man"—will father most of the offspring. Courtship may last for a few hours or up to two or three days. After that, the couple separates. The mother will give birth and raise her baby alone.

Incredible Journey

About one month after mating, the baby is born. Most species of kangaroos give birth to only one baby, although there are occasionally twins. Musky rat kangaroos are the only ones that usually give birth to twins.

Many animals go to a lot of trouble to find and prepare a safe place for their young before they are born. Not the mother kangaroo, however. She has a built-in home for her babies—on her abdomen!

Just before she gives birth the doe cleans her pouch. The newborn kangaroo, or joey, is born outside the pouch. No bigger than a jellybean, it is hairless and blind and almost totally helpless. Its front legs are well developed, however, and the joey uses them to crawl through the fur of its mother's belly, following a trail that she has licked from below her tail to the pouch. Once safely inside the warm pouch, the newborn attaches itself to one of its mother's four nipples and nurses on her milk.

Thanks to its mother's nourishing milk, this quokka joey has grown quickly. Its ears and eyes are now well developed, but for the moment it still seems quite happy to observe the world from the cozy safety of its mother's pouch.

Home Sweet Home

The inside of its mother's dark, warm pocket is the joey's home for the next few months. As time passes the youngster grows fur and develops eyes, ears, back legs and a tail. When the joey is five or more months old, it peeps out at the world for the first time. It cannot reach the ground from inside the pouch but when mom bends down to feed on the grass, the joey nibbles a bit too.

Soon it is time for the joey to try out its legs. At first it only leaves the pouch for short periods, and its mother is careful not to let her baby out of her sight.

Not all joeys are anxious to leave the security of the pouch, however. Sometimes the mother kangaroo has to encourage her young one a bit by bending down and tipping it out onto the ground.

Male and female joeys are about the same size as long as they are living in the pouch. Once they are living outside the pouch, males start growing faster. By the time they are adults, the males may be up to twice the size of females.

Opposite page: *When a joey jumps back into the pouch, it often ends up with its legs sticking out until it gets settled.*

Growing Up

Gradually, the joey begins to spend more time outside the pouch—but it never strays very far. And at the first sign of danger, the young kangaroo dives headfirst back into the pouch, does a complete somersault inside, then peeks outside to see if all is clear!

Joeys are very playful and enjoy wrestling and frolicking with each other. Sometimes they have boxing matches, but these are all in good fun.

As the joey grows the pouch expands, but after about 8 to 10 months the young kangaroo has outgrown its mobile home. It will continue to need its mother's care for some time yet, but even if it wants to return to the pouch she will not let it back in.

At one and a half to two years old, a female kangaroo is ready to start a family of her own. Usually she stays in the mob where she was born, but a young male normally leaves to take up his life as a boomer—and perhaps someday as the ''old man'' in a new mob.

Words to Know

Blue Flier A female red kangaroo which is a blue-gray color and can travel quickly.

Boomer A male kangaroo.

Doe A female kangaroo.

Joey A baby kangaroo.

Macropod From *Macropodidae*, the scientific name for the kangaroo family. Literally, "big foot."

Marsupials A class of mammals whose females carry their young in a pouch until they are fully developed.

Mate To come together to produce young. Either member of an animal pair is also the other's mate.

Mob A herd of kangaroos.

Nipple The part of the mother's body through which a baby drinks her milk.

"Old Man" Leader of a kangaroo mob.

Pouch The fur-lined pocket of the female marsupial where the baby lives until it is fully developed.

Quokka A kind of wallaby found only in a few places in southwestern Australia.

Tendon A tough, strong band or cord of tissue that attaches a muscle to a bone (or to some other part).

INDEX

Cover Photo: Jim Grace (Photo Researchers)

Photo Credits: Heidi Ecker (Focus Stock Photo), page 4; Breck P. Kent, pages 7, 11, 15, 31; John Cancalosi, pages 8, 12-13, 19, 22, 43; Bill Ivy, page 16; Eugen Schuhmacher (WWF-Photolibrary), page 21; Michael Simmons (Focus Stock Photo), page 24; Tom McHugh (Photo Researchers), page 27; Dr. E.R. Degginger, page 28; Len Lee Rue III, pages 32, 36-37; Len Rue Jr., page 40; Dallas Heaton (Canapress/Uniphoto Picture Agency), page 39; Kraseman (Peter Arnold/ Hot Shots), page 45.

OCT. 27 1994 DATE DUE			
SEP 0 5 1995			
JUL 1 6 1996			
MAR 0 7 1998			
JUL 2 1998			
JUL 2 5 1998			
OCT 2 6 2000			
DEC 0 8 2005			
MAR 1 6 2006			
APR 3 0 2012			